HE GIVES YOU PEACE

A Devotional on Finding Peace In Jesus Christ

Doris Willis

ISBN 979-8-89112-049-5 (Paperback)
ISBN 979-8-89112-050-1 (Digital)

Covenant Books
11661 Hwy 707
Murrells Inlet, SC 29576
www.covenantbooks.com

CONTENTS

Introduction...v

The Peace of Knowing the Lord's Everlasting Presence and Protection............................1
The Peace That Guards Your Heart and Mind...4
The Peace That Comes from the Wisdom of Heaven...7
The Peace of Trusting in God—Your Thought Life...11
The Peace That Comes from Trusting God—in Every Situation...................................14
The Gift of Peace That Is Greater Than the World...18
The Gift of Peace That Brings Unity..20
The Gift of Peace That Brings Harmony...23
The Gift of Peace That Can Be Shared...26
The Gift of Peace in Your Conversations...28
The Gift of Peace That Governs Your Life...31
The Gift of Peace That Keeps You from Stumbling...34
The Gift of Peace That Changes Your Focus..37
The Gift of Peace That Equips Us..39
The Gift of Peace That Binds Us...41
The Gift of Peace That Encourages Forgiveness...44
The Gift of Peace That Overcomes the World..47
The Gift of Peace—When Things Don't Go As Expected..49
The Gift of Peace in Faithful Living...52
The Gift of Peace That Flows in Abundance..56
The Gift of Peace That Is Planted in Righteousness...59
The Gift of Peace in the Lord's Safety..62
The Gift of Peace in Daily Conduct...64
The Gift of Peace in the Face of a Friend's Betrayal...66
The Gift of Peace That Can Make Your Spirit Whole...68
The Peace of God That Joins Us Together..71
The Gift of Peace That Blesses..73

INTRODUCTION

Peace is a gift. One of the most sought-after states of being is peace of mind. People spend a tremendous amount of time and resources searching for the thing that will give them peace in culture and society that increasingly thrives on disharmony, chaos, and what seems to be unending crisis.

We change jobs, change career paths, and increase our educational status in an effort to find peace in our work life. We change relationships, change our marital status, and adjust our parenting styles to try to find peace in our home life. We change our lifestyle to become healthier physically, mentally, and emotionally in an effort to find peace. We conduct self-evaluation of our spiritual beliefs, looking for the right path that will lead us to peace.

But the peace we seek is not found in other people, places, or possessions. The peace we seek is found in Jesus Christ. Our Savior came to bring peace by reconciling us to the Father. He left his peace in us through the presence of the Holy Spirit. He told us how to overcome the world—by seeking peace in him.

He Gives You Peace is a devotional of biblical topics on how the peace of God impacts our lives and daily decisions. My prayer is that you will recognize and seek the peace of Jesus Christ as you engage with these devotional studies.

THE PEACE OF KNOWING THE LORD'S EVERLASTING PRESENCE AND PROTECTION

Psalm 121:1–8

Psalm 121 is known as a Song of Ascents or Song of Steps. This chapter is part of a group of chapters that include Psalm 120–134. This is a group of songs for travelers, sung by Hebrew pilgrims on their way up to Jerusalem or while ascending toward Mount Zion or by the priests as they entered the temple.

The theme of this chapter is certainly about trusting the Lord. There is great peace in placing our trust in God, who is always present and who always provides the protection we need as we travel in this journey of life.

Reading the Word

> I lift my eyes toward the mountains.
> Where will my help come from?
> My help comes from the LORD,
> the Maker of heaven and earth.
>
> He will not allow your foot to slip;
> your Protector will not slumber.
> Indeed, the Protector of Israel
> does not slumber or sleep.
>
> The LORD protects you;
> the LORD is a shelter right by your side.
> The sun will not strike you by day
> or the moon by night.

The Lord will protect you from all harm;
He will protect your life.
The Lord will protect your coming and going
both now and forever. (Psalm 121:1–8 HCSB)

Living Word by Word

The Songs of Ascent that Hebrew travelers would sing during their journey were songs of praise and worship. In Psalm 121, the travelers lifted their praise and worship to *Jehovah Ezer*, which means "Lord our help." He is God, who brought the heavens and the earth into existence by his spoken word (Psalm 121:1–2). They praised *Jehovah-Nissi*, who is our keeper and the protector of our souls (Psalm 121:3–7). They praised God because he is always present in every situation (Psalm 121:8).

The pilgrimage was not just a quick day trip and back. The Hebrews had to plan for where they would be able to find food and shelter along the way. They had to travel over rough lands and sometimes encounter dangerous people. They had to protect their families.

The journey may have become tedious, tiring, and even dangerous as they traveled the road to Jerusalem, but the Hebrews could take on their journey with confidence because of their relationship with God.

They had experience with God, and so they could say with assurance that God was their help. The peace was in knowing that the God of Abraham, Isaac, and Jacob was with them on their journey.

In Psalm 121, we read that God is the creator and sustainer of all things. He is the sustainer of his people—providing for the needs of their daily life and for the long journey. His help was not limited to food, clothing, and shelter. He gives strength for daily living and performing daily activities.

He gives grace that enables us to stand strong in the face of challenges, struggles, and successes. He is present in the time of disappointment or despair and in the time of satisfaction and joy. His help is always on time and always in season.

1. What does it mean to you that God is able to sustain you and provide for everything you need for the day and for a lifetime?___________________________

____

____

____

2.   The relationship that the Hebrew worshippers sang about in Psalm 121 was based on a lifetime of knowing God and depending on his grace for living. Read Psalm 121:5–8. What are some practical ways God protects his people throughout their lives? ____

____

____

____

3.   In what ways can you find peace in the knowledge that God is the sustainer and protector of your life? ____

____

____

____

There is great peace in knowing that the Creator of heaven and earth and the one who keeps everything in nature in its place is also able to provide your needs, guide your feet on the path of your life, and protect your soul.

Peace for the Journey

Father, thank you for the peace of knowing that you are my help in every situation in my life. Your grace is sufficient to sustain me, provide for me, and protect me on my daily journey. In the name of Jesus Christ, my Savior, I pray. Amen.

THE PEACE THAT GUARDS YOUR HEART AND MIND

Philippians 4:6–7

In the past few years, it seems that the world has gone through a cycle of chaos and uncertainty. We have been in the front-row seats via the various media to some of the most horrific behaviors, including the senseless loss of life and devastation of communities that have shocked our senses and left us wondering who is in control. We have witnessed the attempted destruction of many values that most of us believe are key to living in a well-structured society. For some, our very faith has been shaken, to the point of a division in our homes, our families, and even in the church, and we are looking for a way to be restored. All these things have challenged our minds and our hearts to try to find a place of peace.

Reading the Word

> Rejoice in the Lord always. Again I say, rejoice! Let everyone see your gentleness. The Lord is near! Do not be anxious about anything. Instead, in every situation, through prayer and petition with thanksgiving, tell your requests to God. And the peace of God that surpasses all understanding will guard your hearts and minds in Christ Jesus. (Philippians 4:4–7 NET)

Living Word by Word

According to the National Institute of Mental Health, an estimated one-fifth of United States adults had an anxiety disorder in the past year. Further, an estimated one-third of US adults experience an anxiety disorder at some time in their lives.[1]

---

[1] National Institute of Mental Health, https://nimh.nih.gov/health/statistics/any-anxiety-disorder.

Christians are not exempt from this issue of anxiety, sometimes to the point of needing to seek mental health counseling. Like others around us, we worry about the many aspects of our lives, including our marriages, family, children, health, finances, jobs, and even how ministry is carried out in the church. Anxiety infiltrates our lives when we are vulnerable, and it invades our thoughts and our attitudes, and if left unchecked, it influences our conduct.

Although we do not discount the value of seeking mental health counseling, the apostle Paul instructs us on the proper way to approach this issue of anxiety from a spiritual perspective.

The apostle Paul, in his letter to the Philippian church, took some time to address how we are to deal with circumstances that bring us to the point of disagreement or division. Paul's advice was to remember where our joy comes from (Philippian 4:4) and demonstrate that joy in the way we deal with one another in the face of difficult situations (Philippians 4:5). And in Philippians 4:6–7, Paul explained how we are to seek the Lord to restore us and to sustain us as we learn to conduct ourselves toward one another and flourish even in difficult times.

In these verses, Paul gives us a two-step process to follow: (a) stop worrying and (b) start praying.

Stop Worrying

In the Sermon on the Mount, Jesus taught that worry comes from placing our faith and our focus on the wrong things. We focus on the things that will meet our needs for food, clothing, shelter, relationships, and personal comfort. And we spend our time trying to accumulate those things on our own, and we worry because we do not have full control of everything that impacts our efforts. We worry about failing in our efforts. Sometimes, we worry that we are not concerned enough about the situation.

Jesus said that above all else, we are to pursue the kingdom of God and his righteousness, and he will provide for all our needs. When we spend our time worrying, we are struggling between establishing our own kingdom or seeking the kingdom of God.

1. What life situation are you worrying about? What could happen if you willingly stop struggling to have your own will and yield yourself to God's will?__________

   ____

   ____

   ____

   ____

Start Praying

In Philippians 4:6, Paul taught that prayer should be the first strategy, not the last resort: "Instead, in every situation, through prayer and petition with thanksgiving, tell your requests to God (verse 6b).

- Prayer allows us to seek God's purpose in a difficult situation (Proverbs 3:6).
- Prayer provides an opportunity for Christians to join with like-minded believers to petition God regarding the situation (1 John 5:14–15).
- Prayer can lift the burden of anxiety as we are ministered to by the Holy Spirit (Romans 8:26–27).
- Prayer helps us cope with the difficult challenges we face in a situation because we have the presence and peace of God (Philippians 4:7).

2. What could change in how you approach life challenges if your first strategy becomes prayer instead of worry?____

____

____

____

____

Will you accept the peace of God that is yours through prayer? It is yours because the Savior promised to give us peace (John 14:27).

> It takes the same amount of energy to worry as it does to pray. One leads to peace and the other leads to panic. (David Jeremiah)

Peace for the Journey

Father, help me to seek your kingdom instead of my own. Thank you for the peace that only you can give to me. Peace like no other. Peace surpasses my understanding. In the name of Jesus Christ, I pray. Amen.

THE PEACE THAT COMES FROM THE WISDOM OF HEAVEN

James 3:17–19

The biblical writer James asked a profound question: "Who is wise and understanding among you?" (James 3:13). Interestingly, he asked this question in a chapter where his focus was on how we conducted ourselves in our speech. His point was that godly wisdom influences the way we conduct ourselves in speech and conversation. Godly wisdom is a representation of your relationship with God, and the it reflects your spiritual growth. Godly wisdom guides and instructs us. It sets the guidelines for what we say and what we do in our interactions and relationships with others. Godly wisdom helps us to walk within those guidelines so that we can live a peaceful life.

Reading the Word

> Who is wise and understanding among you? By his good conduct he should show his works done in the gentleness that wisdom brings. But if you have bitter jealousy and selfishness in your hearts, do not boast and tell lies against the truth. Such wisdom does not come from above but is earthly, natural, demonic. For where there is jealousy and selfishness, there is disorder and every evil practice. But the wisdom from above is first pure, then peaceable, gentle, accommodating, full of mercy and good fruit, impartial, and not hypocritical. And the fruit that consists of righteousness is planted in peace among those who make peace. (James 3:13–18 NET)

Living Word by Word

In James 3:13–18, James offers a clear solution for how we are to manage our conduct, especially in what we say. We can learn some important facts from this passage about wisdom. James taught about the elements of ungodly wisdom (James 3:14–16), the characteristics of godly wisdom (James 3:17), and the benefit of choosing godly wisdom (James 3:18).

Characteristics of Ungodly Wisdom

> But if you have bitter jealousy and selfishness in your hearts, do not boast and tell lies against the truth. Such wisdom does not come from above but is earthly, natural, demonic. For where there is jealousy and selfishness, there is disorder and every evil practice. (James 3:14–16 NET)

1. According to verse 14, ungodly wisdom is evident in an attitude of bitter jealousy and selfishness. He mentions two specific behaviors that one who has this attitude would demonstrate. What are those behaviors? This person would ________________ and tell __________ against the truth.

2. What does James say is the source of this ungodly wisdom (verse 15)? __________

____

____

____

____

3. What is the result of the presence of jealousy and selfishness (verse 16)? ________

____

____

____

____

Characteristics of Godly Wisdom

> But the wisdom from above is first pure, then peaceable, gentle, accommodating, full of mercy and good fruit, impartial, and not hypocritical. (James 3:17 NET)

In James 3:17, the writer describes for us what godly wisdom looks like in the life of a Christian. In contrast to the wisdom that is from fleshly desires, the wisdom of heaven reflects the righteousness of God.

- This wisdom is pure, that is, the opposite of bitter jealousy and selfishness.
- This wisdom is peaceful. It does not seek to cause disorder (chaos) and strife.
- This wisdom is gentle (patient) and accommodating (adjusting my own needs to consider the needs of others).
- This wisdom is full of mercy (compassionate, bearing up for one another's weaknesses).
- This wisdom is impartial (it does not show favoritism; it is unwavering and reliable).
- This wisdom is not hypocritical (it is transparent, sincere, and humble).

The Benefit of Choosing Godly Wisdom

> And the fruit that consists of righteousness is planted in peace among those who make peace. (James 3:18 NET)

In James 3:18, James encourages us with the news that when we choose godly wisdom, our speech reflects the righteousness of Jesus Christ, and our speech and lives will reflect his peace. Not only can we enjoy the peace of God in our own lives, but we can also encourage others to seek his peace as well.

4. In what way can you demonstrate godly wisdom in your life? _______________
____
____
____
____

5. How can you encourage growing in godly wisdom in others? _______________
____
____
____
____

When we choose to grow spiritually in godly wisdom, our life's focus changes, beginning with the heart. The change is evident in our thinking, our attitudes, our conversation, and our conduct. The change is reflected in our humility and in compassion. This day-by-day change in our hearts brings us the peace of God.

Peace for the Journey

Father, thank you for the wisdom that comes from heaven. Help me to seek it and apply it to my life, day by day. Thank you for the peace of godly wisdom. In the name of Jesus Christ, I pray. Amen.

THE PEACE OF TRUSTING IN GOD—YOUR THOUGHT LIFE

Isaiah 26:3

What thoughts seem to occupy your mind most of the time? Are you thinking about issues in your home, your marriage, your family, your career, and your relationships with others? Do you find yourself worrying about these issues and wondering how they will be resolved? Are you seeking the counsel of God's Word and the comfort of his Holy Spirit? Are you trusting him instead of your own understanding? Our passage states that God will give you perfect peace, that is, the peace of peace if you keep your mind on him and trust in him.

Reading the Word

> You will keep in perfect peace
> all who trust in you,
> all whose thoughts are fixed on you! (Isaiah 26:3 NLT)

Living Word by Word

In Isaiah 26:3, the words *perfect peace* comes from the Hebrew *shalom, shalom,* translated as "peace, peace" or peace upon peace—all kinds of prosperity—happiness in this world and in the world to come.[2]

Webster's dictionary offers the following definition for perfect peace: freedom from disquieting or oppressive thoughts or emotions.[3]

Our Savior will keep us in perfect peace as we abide in him (John 15:4–11). The Bible gives us other guidance in how to live in the "peace, peace" of God.

---

[2] Clarke, Adam, "Commentary on Isaiah 26:3," *The Adam Clarke Commentary* (1832), https://www.studylight.org/commentaries/acc/isaiah-26.html.

[3] Merriam-Webster, Incorporated, https://www.merriam-webster.com/dictionary/peace, 2023.

The scriptures provide a plan for keeping your mind on Jesus Christ in challenging times. Here are a few quick pointers for focusing on him and receiving his peace for your life.

1. *Just because you think a thing does not make it true.* Our minds are constantly bombarded with information. Do not be surprised that much of that information is meant to draw you away from your faith in God and your understanding of the scriptures. Search the scriptures to see how the "facts" of the world align with the truth of God (John 5:39–47, 2 Timothy 3:16–17).

2. *Just because you desire it does not mean it is God's plan for your life.* The world offers many opportunities for each of us to define the direction of our lives. Community and cultural input can influence what you believe about your options. But only the Word of God can lead you to God's purpose for you (Jeremiah 29:11, 33:3; Isaiah 30:21; 1 Timothy 2:3–4; James 1:5).

3. *Just because it sounds like the best thing to do does not mean it is the best thing for you.* Trust God to set the direction for your life. The challenges will still be involved, and life may still present some difficult situations that you will overcome. But when you are following him and your mind is focused on him, his direction will lead you to successful living and peace of mind—every time (Proverbs 3:5–6).

Think it through

1. How can seeking the peace of God instead of your own understanding make a difference in your thought life? ____

____

____

____

2. What attitudes have you developed about your life that are influenced mainly by the culture of your community and that influence how you live in peace?________

____

____

____

3. How do these attitudes you listed in the previous question affect your decision making? ____

____

____

____

____

4. How do those attitudes shape your reactions and responses in uncomfortable situation? ____

____

____

____

____

5. How do these attitudes impact the peace of your heart?_______________________

____

____

____

____

Peace for the Journey

Father, thank you for the peace that you give. I will focus on you as my source of peace. In the name of Jesus Christ, I pray. Amen.

THE PEACE THAT COMES FROM TRUSTING GOD— IN EVERY SITUATION

Psalm 46

One of the great disrupters of our peace is the constantly changing ideologies of the world. It seems that what was considered right, true, and appropriate in the past is now cast aside by an "enlightened" society and considered incorrect and inappropriate. These constant changes place barriers of contention between spouses, between parents and children, among extended families, and within educational institutions, the workplace, communities, and cultures—and even in the church. Ideological indecisiveness leads governments and nations to be at odds, and, in some cases, even leads to war. This constant state of strife and chaos impacts our peace of mind and our peace of heart.

Who can we trust to have our best interest in mind in every situation? I have some good news for you. The Word of God declares that we have a God who is our safe hiding place and our strong defense when the world is falling apart around us. Trust God to preserve the peace of your heart.

Reading the Word

> God is our strong refuge;
> he is truly our helper in times of trouble.
> For this reason we do not fear when the earth shakes,
> and the mountains tumble into the depths of the sea,
> when its waves crash and foam,
> and the mountains shake before the surging sea. (Selah)
> The river's channels bring joy to the city of God,
> the special, holy dwelling place of the Most High.

God lives within it, it cannot be moved.
God rescues it at the break of dawn.
Nations are in uproar, kingdoms are overthrown.
God gives a shout, the earth dissolves.
The LORD of Heaven's Armies is on our side.
The God of Jacob is our stronghold.
Come, Witness the exploits of the LORD,
who brings devastation to the earth.
He brings an end to wars throughout the earth.
He shatters the bow and breaks the spear;
he burns the shields with fire.
He says, "Stop your striving and recognize that I am God.
I will be exalted over the nations! I will be exalted over the earth!"
The LORD of Heaven's Armies is on our side!
The God of Jacob is our stronghold! (Selah) (Psalm 46:1–11 NET)

Living Word by Word

Psalm 46 is a psalm about trusting God. We can trust him when the very elements of the world seem to be out of control—in the face of storms and floods, in earthquakes, and in the path of destructive waters. Our God is in control of all of these, and he can turn the forces of these elements for our good. When the storms in our lives seem to be out of control, we can trust God to move on our behalf when we submit ourselves to him.

1. What life issue is causing a storm in your mind and heart? _________________

____

____

____

____

2. How has your faith been tested because of this current challenge? _____________

____

____

____

____

3. How can knowing that God is a safe place and a place of protection give you peace of mind and heart as you deal with this current challenge? _______________________

____

____

____

The world we live in goes through cycles of peace and war, calm and chaos, and alternately preserving our values and destroying them. Psalm 46:6–10 declares that the Lord is in control even when the nations are in a state of mass confusion, strife, and chaos. Verse 7 states that "the Lord of hosts" is with those who are called by his great name and those who have a spiritual relationship with him. Even during the utter downfall of the nations, God will not leave his people without protection. He is our El Shaddai—our strong defense.

1. God can end all wars—even the emotional, mental, and spiritual wars—forever. What strife and chaos in your life is keeping you from experiencing the peace of God? ____

____

____

____

2. What steps can you take to give God control over the order in your life and allow him to give you peace of mind and heart? _______________________________

____

____

____

Our God is not only our safe place and our defense, but he is also the one who judges the earth and all that is in it.

When you are dealing with life matters that are challenging your faith and your peace, it is often difficult to be still. Sometimes, you may literally find yourself pacing the floor to find an answer to the situation. In Psalm 46:10–11, we are reminded that God is almighty. He can handle everything that concerns you.

And he is ultimately the judge of your life and of all the earth. You are his child, by the blood of Jesus Christ, so you can trust him to do what is right on your behalf.

To "be still" means to live with an assurance that God is sovereign over all. Whatever the situation—no matter how dire it looks from your point of view, God will deal with it on your behalf according to his own purpose and plan for your life. His plans do not change because of changes in political, social, or cultural norms. He is immutable, omnipotent, omniscient, and omnipresent.

Peace for the Journey

Father, thank you for the peace that I have in knowing that I can trust you as my safe hiding place and my strong defense. Thank you for working out every situation for my good. In the name of Jesus Christ, I pray. Amen.

THE GIFT OF PEACE THAT IS GREATER THAN THE WORLD

John 14:27

The common Eastern salutation used in both gathering, together with one another and departing from one another, is peace—"Shalom, Shalom." *Shalom* is a Hebrew word that means peace, harmony, prosperity, welfare, and tranquility in your life. But it is more than just health, wealth, and happiness. It refers to a sense of inward wholeness or completeness. It is more than just the absence of conflict in your life. It encompasses a wellness in the spirit. It conveys a blessing of well-being.

Reading the Word

> Peace I leave with you; my peace I give to you. Not as the world gives do I give to you. Let not your hearts be troubled, neither let them be afraid. (John 14:27 ESV)

Living Word by Word

Chapter 14 might be considered the comfort chapter in the Gospel of John. It begins with the Lord assuring his disciples of who he is and what his mission was on behalf of those who believe in him (John 14:1–4, 6). Jesus reminded them that he and the Father are on one accord. Jesus is the exact representation of the Father (John 14:7, 9–11). He promised a helper (Paraclete) to abide with those who believe in him forever (John 14:16–18, 26). And he promised his peace (John 14:27), a legacy of peace that can remove fear and worry from our hearts—a peace like no other!

A *legacy* can be defined as a gift that is passed down from one generation to another. Parents pass down gifts of property and investments to their children and grandchildren. Christian parents also strive to pass down a legacy of godly character and faith. Jesus promised a legacy of peace. It was a gift and a promise that remains eternally. It is not a casual wish for peace but a certainty of his peace as we abide in him. It is a peace that cannot be duplicated by the world. It is the only lasting peace, and it is only found in Jesus Christ.

1. In what area of your life do you need to feel the peace (shalom) of God? ________

____

____

____

____

2. How can you build a legacy of peace for your family? ________________

____

____

____

____

Peace for the Journey

Father, thank you for the legacy of peace that you have given to those who abide in you. Teach us how to live our lives to leave a legacy of peace for our children and grandchildren. In the name of Jesus Christ, I pray. Amen.

THE GIFT OF PEACE THAT BRINGS UNITY

Colossians 3:15

In every season of life, we find that we must change our behavior in order to embrace our new status. When a young couple goes from being single and dating to being married, they leave behind the behaviors of an unmarried couple and put on the qualities of a husband and wife. They are no longer two separate entities but are united as one body. Their thoughts and habits are no longer what pleased each of them as individual singles. Now, they must make decisions based on what is best for their new family. So the traits they exhibit in their new roles must be demonstrated in how they care for one another, how they speak to one another, and how they forgive one another so that they can dwell together in unity and peace.

Reading the Word

> Let the peace of Christ rule in your hearts, since as members of one
> body you were called to peace. And be thankful. (Colossians 3:15 NIV)

Living Word by Word

In Colossians chapter 3, the apostle Paul wrote about the worldly behaviors that followers of Jesus Christ are to take off and the Christlike behaviors we are to put on if we are to live in holiness and unity in Jesus Christ. Paul was specific in his list of behaviors that represent the fleshly nature in Colossians 3:5–9: sensuality, evil attitudes, evil speech, and deception. Paul called this the behavior of the "old man" and said that those who proclaim Jesus Christ must not practice these behaviors.

Note that Paul said that we are to put these behaviors to death. The idea is that we do not just set them aside. There will not be a convenient time to take them up again if we are walking in Jesus Christ. We will no longer need nor desire these behaviors as part of our life in Jesus Christ. These behaviors offer no lasting peace, and they cause disunity and separation in our relationship with Jesus Christ and in our relationships with others. It is a daily calling to set aside these behaviors because we still live in a natural body. We will be tempted because there is evil in the world, but the evidence of our walk in Christ is that we do not take up the old man again.

In Colossians 3:11–14, Paul defined the character traits that followers of Christ are to put on as the "new man." First of all, he indicated that we have to change how we think of ourselves—no more sons of disobedience (3:6) but as the "elect of God," "holy" and "beloved."

In this new status, followers of Christ must embrace new character traits. Colossians 3:12–14 lists the new traits we are to put on: compassion, kindness, humility, gentleness, patience, and love. These "new man" traits are not meant to cover over the old traits but to supplant them and remove them from our lives. It is also a daily calling to put on and demonstrate these traits in our lives.

Paul also provided counsel on how the Holy Spirit will minister to us daily as we strive to live as the "new man." In Colossians 3:15–17, he spoke of three sources of strength and lasting peace that brings unity for the body of Christ:

(1) *Let the peace of God rule in our hearts.* Ruling our hearts has the idea of governing our hearts so that we walk in godly boundaries for our lives. This peace also serves as an arbitrator of our hearts so that we correctly weigh or reason out the desires of our hearts. It signifies a change of attitude. The peace of God instills a sense of well-being and wholeness, even when there is conflict and disunity happening around us.

(2) *Let the word of God dwell richly in us.* The word of God provides godly principles for how we are to think, behave, and speak in our "new man" daily walk. It represents a change in our decision making. As we read the Word of God, the Holy Spirit will teach it to our hearts and will counsel us on how to live it in fellowship with Jesus Christ and in our fellowship and interactions with others.

(3) *Honor God in all that you do and be thankful.* Our whole life is to be a testimony of the grace of God through Jesus Christ toward us. It requires a change in our habits. Our thoughts, conversations, acts, worship, work, home life, school life, and relationships should be carried out with an attitude of honoring God.

1. Unity is important in the church—the body of Christ. But it is also important in your home. Which of the "old man" traits do you need to put off daily so you can walk in unity in your home?____

____

____

____

____

2. Which of the "new man" traits are a challenge for you to embrace? ___________

____

____

____

____

Peace for the Journey

Father, thank you for the peace of Jesus Christ that brings unity and is not disrupted by the chaos of the world, but is everlasting and dwells in us by the presence of your Holy Spirit. Amen.

THE GIFT OF PEACE THAT BRINGS HARMONY

Romans 15:5–6

Harmony and peace. Each of us, at some point, searches for and desires these two elements to be present in our life. In this passage, Paul addresses how believers can walk together and support one another—the strong walking alongside and encouraging the weak.

Reading the Word

> May the God of endurance and encouragement grant you to live in such harmony with one another, in accord with Christ Jesus, that together you may with one voice glorify the God and Father of our Lord Jesus Christ. (Romans 15:5–6 ESV)

Living Word by Word

In Romans 15, Paul summarizes the teaching from the previous chapter, where he instructs those who are strong in their faith to receive those who are weak in their faith, without disputing about matters of personal conviction. The discussion revolves around matters of conscience and of liberties that believers have in Jesus Christ, and not matters of walking in righteousness. In Romans 14, Paul taught about how we are to nurture our relationships when there is a difference of personal opinion:

A. Do not spend time disagreeing over matters that are not important to how we honor God in our lives. Paul was teaching about some issues that had arisen in the church among the believers (for example, whether or not to eat meat). Paul taught this is a matter of personal conviction.
B. Don't spend time judging Christians who have different views than your own about matters of personal conviction.

C. Don't spend time arguing about which days you will celebrate as holy days or ceremonial days. Romans 14:2 states that each person must make up his own mind about the celebrations where he will participate.

D. Do not behave toward one another in such a way as to be a stumbling block (causing someone to do something against their personal convictions because it is what you choose to do).

E. Remember that each of us must give account of our conduct to the Lord.

1. Are there some areas where you have sacrificed peace and harmony by disagreeing about matters of personal conviction that are not important to how you honor God in your life? ____

____

____

____

____

Paul also refers to those who are weak in their faith and those who are strong in their faith. In Chapter 15, Paul taught that those who are strong should encourage those who are weak. It's important to understand what it means to be strong in your faith.

Christians grow strong in faith by learning to apply biblical truths to their lives and developing the habit of practicing those truths in their relationships with others (Joshua 1:8; 2 Timothy 2:15; 2 Timothy 3:16–17). Growing stronger in faith includes how we grow in relationship with one another. Those who are growing in their faith (a) walk in humility before the Lord (James 4:10) and among others (Ephesians 4:2); (b) treat others with respect, including respecting their personal convictions (1 Peter 2:17; Romans 12:10); (c) demonstrate Christlike compassion, kindness, and forgiveness toward others; and (d) encourage others to grow in their faith with wisdom by living a lifestyle that is of genuineness, honesty, and trustworthiness. In Romans 14:19, we read that growing strong in our faith in this way would lead to peace and to the edification of one another.

2. Which of these biblical truths listed in the paragraph above can you embrace to bring peace and harmony to your relationships?____

____

____

____

____

When we pursue harmony and peace, every area of our lives is impacted. Our physical well-being is improved because of reduced stress levels. Our emotional health is strengthened because we can focus our energy on developing stronger relationships, instead of building a defensive wall. Our spiritual health is increased when we seek the counsel of the Holy Spirit in our relationships.

Peace for the Journey

Father, thank you for the gift of harmony and peace that comes in our relationship with Jesus Christ.

THE GIFT OF PEACE THAT CAN BE SHARED

Reading the Word

> Blessed are the peacemakers, for they will be called children of God. (Matthew 5:9 NIV)

Living Word by Word

Matthew 5:9 is the seventh of the beatitudes we find in the Sermon of the Mount. Each of the beatitudes addresses a characteristic that followers of Jesus Christ are expected to exhibit. Verse 9 focuses on the characteristic of being a peacemaker. Peacemakers do not just talk about peace; they pursue a lifestyle that creates an environment of peace. Their attitudes toward people and situations are influenced by the desire to create peace. Their conversations are built around words that encourage peace. Their opinions are expressed in a way to foster peace. Their actions are meant to demonstrate peace. The pursuit of peace begins with the one who desires peace—the peacemaker. Peacemakers have some specific character traits.

- Peacemakers do not avoid conflict. Their approach is to look for and offer solutions that promote peace.
- Peacemakers readily seek forgiveness and offer forgiveness to others. They look for ways to avoid holding grudges and to bring reconciliation when it is possible.
- Peacemakers respect others' point of view. They embrace an environment where all are encouraged to speak the truth. But they will not compromise the truth by accepting popular or cultural beliefs over God's Word.

The one who seeks godly peace will embody the other characteristics of humility (v. 3), a repentant heart (v. 4), self-control (v. 5), mercy toward others (v. 6), and seekers of righteousness (v. 7). If seeking peace and maintaining peace is an objective for your life, you must be an active peace seeker.

Do you want to talk about peace, or are you willing to reach out to others to pursue peace in your relationships?

1. In what ways do you feel the peace of Jesus Christ in your life? _______________
    ____
    ____
    ____
    ____

2. In what ways are you pursuing peace in your relationships?_______________
    ____
    ____
    ____
    ____

Pursuing a life of peace begins with your relationship in Jesus Christ. He is the one who gives peace to overcome every life challenge (John 16:33). It is a peace we can embrace and share in all our relationships.

Peace for the Journey

Father, thank you for the peace that we have in Jesus Christ. Help us to pursue godly peace in our thoughts, our attitudes, our conversations, and our actions. In the name of Jesus Christ, I pray. Amen.

THE GIFT OF PEACE IN YOUR CONVERSATIONS

When you are striving to be part of a united team, your words and your conversations matter in the pursuit of peace and harmony. Encouraging words, positive and upbeat, go a long way toward creating an environment where people want to be engaged. Whether the conversation is in the church, in your home, or in your workplace environment, everyone appreciates words that bring peace. Peaceful words, especially in times of conflict or high stress, help to create a space in which agreement and comradeship can thrive.

Reading the Word

> For, "Whoever would love life and see good days must keep their tongue from evil and their lips from deceitful speech. They must turn from evil and do good; they must seek peace and pursue it." (1 Peter 3:10–11 NIV)

Living Word by Word

It is notable that the writer of 1 Peter included these verses right after his admonition to husbands and wives about how they are to submit to, honor, and respect one another. Peter's instruction in this chapter goes from the specific (husbands/wives) to the general (all of you). He focuses on how Christians are to address one another and treat one another. Christians are to demonstrate love for one another, desiring unity of spirit, and showing compassion, gentleness, and humility in our relationships with one another. We are to behave this way so that we can be a blessing to one another and we may inherit a blessing in Jesus Christ (v. 9).

The opposite of an attitude that brings blessings is one that stirs up division and disunity. This is the attitude and behavior that returns "evil for evil" or gives "insult for insult." Peter brings this up because it is a work of the flesh, and if we are not careful, we can be tempted to respond in this way. Evil and deceitful speech refers to any kind of speech that is meant to twist or manipulate information or tear down a person or a situation. Deceitful speech is words that give a false impression to influence or control the attitudes or behaviors of others. Evil and deceitful speech is divisive and destructive and an enemy of peace.

1. Peter reminds us of the goal for our lives if we are to "love life and see good days" (v. 10). List those goals here:
   a. Refrain my tongue from _________________.
   b. Keep my lips from speaking _________________.
   c. Turn away from _________________ and do _____________________.
   d. Seek _________________ and _________________ it.

In verse 12, Peter reminds us why Christians are to honor God in our speech and conduct toward one another. He tells us that God takes notice of our behavior toward one another, whether it demonstrates righteousness or evil. God takes notice of our prayers, and he is quick to respond to the prayers of the righteous.

Peter's challenging goals in 1 Peter 3:8 provides a daily task list of behaviors for walking together as brothers and sisters in Jesus Christ.

1. *Desire and nurture unity in the Spirit.* This verse has the idea of walking in the counsel of the Holy Spirit together as believers so that our interactions and conduct will honor God and lead us to peaceful lives together. Are there relationships you feel disconnected instead of walking in unity? What can you do to begin restoring the unity in those relationships? ____

   ____

   ____

   ____

2. *Be compassionate toward one another.* Christians are encouraged to be transparent in dealing with one another, empathetic and kind, and gracious and considerate. Is there someone in your circle for whom you can show greater compassion in your day-to-day interactions? How can you start? _________________________

   ____

   ____

   ____

3. *Love one another.* Christian love does not wait to be approached. It reaches out to embrace. It does not stand by waiting to be called upon. It lowers its shoulder to lift up another believer. Is your love toward other Christians approachable? Embraceable? Uplifting? What can you do to be more transparent in your relationships?____

____

____

____

____

4. *Be tenderhearted.* Recognize that all of us have faults and broken places. Offer comfort. Speak the truth in wisdom and love. Seek peace. What can you do in your daily walk to demonstrate tenderheartedness?___________________________________

____

____

____

____

5. *Be courteous and respect one another.* Walk together to encourage spiritual growth—not to pass judgment. We are all a work in progress. Your conversation is not just your words; it includes your attitude toward others. What would you change about your conversation to be more respectful of others?___________________________________

____

____

____

____

Peace for the Journey

Father, help us to strengthen our relationships with others as we strive to walk in the counsel of the Holy Spirit together. Teach us to pursue peace in our everyday conversations. In the name of Jesus Christ, I pray. Amen.

THE GIFT OF PEACE THAT GOVERNS YOUR LIFE

Romans 8:6

The mind governed by the flesh is death, but the mind governed by the Spirit is life and peace.

In Romans Chapter 8, the apostle Paul pronounced a declaration of freedom for those who have been set free in Jesus Christ. He stated that the mindset of those who are free in Jesus Christ is governed by the Holy Spirit and will not be overcome by the yearnings of the flesh but will live a victorious life filled with peace.

Reading the Word

> Therefore, there is now no condemnation for those in Christ Jesus, because the law of the Spirit of life in Christ Jesus has set you free from the law of sin and death. For what the law could not do since it was weakened by the flesh, God did. He condemned sin in the flesh by sending his own Son in the likeness of sinful flesh as a sin offering, in order that the law's requirement would be fulfilled in us who do not walk according to the flesh but according to the Spirit. For those who live according to the flesh have their minds set on the things of the flesh, but those who live according to the Spirit have their minds set on the things of the Spirit. Now the mindset of the flesh is death, but the mindset of the Spirit is life and peace. (Romans 8:1–6 HCSB)

Living Word by Word

This passage of scripture concludes by contrasting the mindset of the flesh (your will, thoughts, emotions, values, and self-focused desires) that results in conflict and that leads to spiritual death with the mindset of the Holy Spirit (desires the righteousness of God, cooperates with the work of the Holy Spirit, and is governed by the Holy Spirit) that leads to a life filled with spiritual peace.

This is not a peace that we can obtain on our own. Read Paul's explanation in Romans 8:1–5 of how we became heirs to the freedom we have in Jesus Christ and this life of peace:

> So now there is no condemnation for those who belong to Christ Jesus. And because you belong to him, the power of the life-giving Spirit has freed you from the power of sin that leads to death. The law of Moses was unable to save us because of the weakness of our sinful nature. So God did what the law could not do. He sent his own Son in a body like the bodies we sinners have. And in that body God declared an end to sin's control over us by giving his Son as a sacrifice for our sins. He did this so that the just requirement of the law would be fully satisfied for us, who no longer follow our sinful nature but instead follow the Spirit. Those who are dominated by the sinful nature think about sinful things, but those who are controlled by the Holy Spirit think about things that please the Spirit. Romans 8:1–6 (NLT)

Paul reaffirms our freedom in Jesus Christ in these scriptures. Read each of them, and record your thoughts in the space provided.

1. Romans 6:2—How were we set free from the law of sin and death? ____________
    ____
    ____
    ____

2. Romans 5:5—What is the mindset of those who live according to the Spirit? ____
    ____
    ____
    ____

3. Romans 8:5—When we are focused on our own emotions, values, and desires, we are being governed by the spirit of the ______________________________.

4. Romans 6:6—What is the result of living in the mindset of the Holy Spirit? _____

____

____

____

____

Peace for the Journey

Father, thank you that you have already defeated the enemy of my soul through the work of your Son, Jesus Christ. Help me to walk in the mindset of the Holy Spirt so that I will not be overcome by the desires of my flesh. In the name of Jesus Christ, I pray. Amen.

THE GIFT OF PEACE THAT KEEPS YOU FROM STUMBLING

Reading the Word

> Jesus said to his disciples: "Things that cause people to stumble are bound to come, but woe to anyone through whom they come. It would be better for them to be thrown into the sea with a millstone tied around their neck than to cause one of these little ones to stumble." (Luke 17:1–2 NIV)

> Great peace have those who love your law, and nothing can make them stumble. (Psalm 119:165 NIV)

The Hebrew word *mikshol*[4] for "stumbling block" has the idea of stubbing a toe against something in such a way that you may stumble or falter when you walk. Strong's Concordance offers this definition of stumbling block: obstacle, enticement, something that caused to fall, gives offence, brings to ruin.

Living Word by Word

I have been the victim of a stubbed toe. I didn't intentionally hit my toe against the foot of the bed; it happened accidentally because I was not watching my path. I know the pain it can cause as that small member of my body seemed to alert every nerve in the rest of my body in such a way that I was totally preoccupied until I dealt with the pain I felt in my toe. The pain was distracting and took my attention away from what I should have been doing. It affected my mood and could potentially affect how I responded to others if I allowed my

---

[4] Strong's Concordance, 4383.

current feelings to control my behavior. It was a small inconvenience for me, but it could have become a bigger issue based on how I chose to respond.

The act of stubbing your toe can cause great distress depending on your response. From a spiritual perspective, a Christian can stub a toe by choosing the wrong response in their conversation or an inappropriate choice of actions or activities. Christians can cause others to stumble by behaving in a way that leads another to act against personal convictions. The key to avoiding the stumbling block is to walk firmly in the Word of God.

A spiritual stumble can have much the same effect if it is not recognized and if the behavior is not corrected.

These are some behaviors that can cause you to stumble:

- Overindulging (food, drink, activities)
- Participating in gossip or passing on gossip you have received
- Habitual lying
- Stretching the truth to make yourself or the circumstances look better
- Perverting the truth to make someone else look bad
- Reacting in anger at remarks made by others
- Using sarcasm or rude remarks to "get even" with someone
- Nurturing a close personal relationship with someone other than your spouse and sharing confidential personal information that should only be shared with your spouse. Such a relationship creates vulnerability between the parties that can lead to intimacy, which results in a negative impact on marriages.

Christians can also cause others to stumble by participating in activities that lead others to act against their own convictions. Social drinking and overeating are examples that are often referred to when we think of causing someone to stumble. While drinking is not in inherently evil, the Bible warns against drunkenness and gluttony (Isaiah 5:11, Proverbs 23:21, Romans 13:13, Ephesians 5:18, and 1 Corinthians 6:10, to list a few). Many people do not drink because they are opposed to drinking for religious reasons or because they are not physically or emotionally able to handle strong drink. The one who seeks to impose their own desires to overindulge in food or drink on those who are opposed to eating or drinking to excess is not only being disrespectful of that person's choices, but also, by insisting that they indulge, can cause them to stumble and act in a way that is contrary to their own convictions.

How shall we live so that we do not cause others to stumble? Paul gives some good advice in his letter to the Roman church: "Therefore let us pursue the things which make for peace and the things by which one may edify another" (Romans 14:19 NKJV).

We are all faced with things that have the potential to tempt us to make decisions that can lead to a stumped toe and can cause us to lead others to stumble as well. Keeping watch over the attitude of our heart, the theme of our conversations, and our personal behavior to walk in a manner worthy of our Savior Jesus Christ. Jesus sent the Holy Spirit to dwell in the hearts of believers so that we would have an everlasting counselor to help us in our daily walk.

1. The Holy Spirit can help us to recognize the situation where we may be tempted and to look for the way to escape. Read 1 Corinthians 10:13. What were some of the sinful behaviors that the people stumbled into as they traveled toward the promised land (verses 6–10). ____

    ____

    ____

    ____

2. In 1 Corinthians 10:13, the writer tells us that we will be tempted. How are we told that we can remain strong under temptation? _______________________________

    ____

3. Temptation will often present itself when we are spiritually, physically, mentally, and emotionally tired. Read the following verses, and write what you learn about God's provision of strength when we feel like we have nothing left to keep moving forward.
    2 Corinthians 12:9 ____
    2 Timothy 1:7 ____
    2 Peter 1:4 ____
    Jude 1:24–25 ____

Peace for the Journey

Father, thank you for the assurance of strength that you will provide so that we are able to stand strong in the presence of the "stumbling" moments. It is you who is able to make a way out. You will keep us from stumbling. You will present us blameless before the presence of your glory with great joy. And we are grateful for your loving kindness toward us. In the name of Jesus Christ, I pray. Amen.

THE GIFT OF PEACE THAT CHANGES YOUR FOCUS

Reading the Word

> Come children. Listen to me.
> I will teach you what it means to fear the LORD.
> Do you want to really live?
> Would you love to live a long, happy life?
> Then make sure you don't speak evil words
> or use deceptive speech.
> Turn away from evil and do what is right.
> Strive for peace and promote it. (Psalm 34:11–14 NET)

Living Word by Word.

King David made a passionate plead to the people of Israel to trust the Lord with reverential fear. In Psalm 34:11–14, he taught the people that reverence for God includes the focus of their heart, minds, and conduct.

- *Reverent fear of the Lord leads to abundant life* (vv. 11–12)
  - Abundant life is a life of right focus.
  - Right focus leads to a fruitful and fulfilling life.
  - Right focus is evident in a change of thinking, of attitude, and of conduct (v. 13).
  - A peaceful life requires active participation in your life—not withdrawal.
- *A change of focus is evident in your speech* (v. 13)
  - Focus on what is best—speak about those things. Not what is popular, culturally comfortable, or politically correct (Philippians 4:8). Keep moving toward

the things that bring godly peace (forgiveness, mercy, grace, and reconciliation). Don't go back to "remember when" (v. 14).

- ○ Write out Philippians 4:8 here. Begin to memorize this scripture and apply it
  in your life. ____
  ____
  ____
  ____
  ____

- *A change of focus changes your attitude.* Fill in the command in verse 13 here: "turn
  from _______________ and do ___________________. Sometimes, we take
  the wrong thinking and run with it to our own defeat and to the detriment of
  others.
- *A change of focus changes your conduct.* "Seek peace and pursuit it" (v. 14). Change
  of focus often comes in small steps.
  - ○ The first step is *self-evaluation.* Where do I need to change my focus so I can
    pursuit peace in my life and relationships?
  - ○ Self-evaluation should lead to the second step of *personal preparation.* What
    knowledge or counsel do I need to seek? What skills or abilities do I need to
    improve, sharpen, or strengthen to change my spiritual focus?
  - ○ Personal preparation should lead to taking *action.* You do not want just to seek
    peace—you want to be a pursuer of peace.
  - ○ *Becoming a peace pursuer* is not a status to be obtained but a lifestyle to embrace.

Peace for the Journey

Father, create in me a heart that desires to pursuit a lifestyle of peace. Help me to focus
my heart on the things that matter to you so that my thoughts and attitude align with your
purpose for me, and my actions reflect your work in me to make me fruitful and fulfilled
according to your will and bring about your glory in my life. In the name of Jesus Christ, I
pray. Amen.

THE GIFT OF PEACE
THAT EQUIPS US

Reading the Word

> Now may the God of peace, who through the blood of the eternal covenant brought back from the dead our Lord Jesus, that great Shepherd of the sheep, equip you with everything good for doing his will, and may he work in us what is pleasing to him, through Jesus Christ, to whom be glory for ever and ever. Amen. (Hebrews 13:20–21 NIV)

Living Word by Word

How many times have you looked at the assigned project at your workplace and thought it was insurmountable? You felt you were unlikely to meet the deadline because the scope was more than you could cover in the time allotted. Or maybe it was a ministry commitment that you later find out had a conflict with another important family engagement. All of us find ourselves juggling our time and resources to meet all of the requests made of us. Sometimes, you may feel that if you cannot meet each commitment with the same elegant style, then it is better to do nothing. But I encourage you to continue to hold on because as a believer in Jesus Christ, you are able to do all that Jesus Christ has purposed for you. He has equipped you for everything that a believer needs for a successful life, a peace-filled life, and a life that brings glory to God.

The writer of Hebrews tells us in this passage that our God has the power to equip us and the desire that we should be equipped. How does our Lord equip us? Read the scriptures below and complete the verses:

1. He has provided his word in 2 Timothy 3:16–17 NET: "Every scripture is inspired by God and useful for _______________, for _______________, for

_________________, and for training in _________________, that the person dedicated to God may be capable and _________________ for every good work."

2. He has provided us the resource of prayer in Psalm 145:18 (NET) so that we can grow closer to God. It says, "The LORD is near all who cry out to him, all who cry out to him _________________."

3. Our prayers give strength and hope in the Lord. In ourselves, we are weak and failing in our attempts to succeed, but when we hope in the Lord, he is our strength. Psalm 73:26 (NET) says, "My flesh and my heart may grow _________________, but God always protects my _________________ and gives me _________________."

4. When we pray to the Lord, we can gain wisdom for decision making and choosing the right course of action when we ask with faith. In James 1:5–6 NET, it says, "But if anyone is _________________ in wisdom, he should ask God, who gives to all _________________ and without reprimand, and it will be given to him. But he must ask in _________________ without doubting, for the one who doubts is like a wave of the sea, blown and tossed around by the wind."

5. The Lord gave gifts to the body of Christ to help us grow up in Christlikeness and maturity. In Ephesians 4:12–16 NET, it says, "to equip the saints for the _________________ of ministry, that is, to build up the body of Christ, until we all attain to the _________________ of the faith and of the _________________ of the Son of God—a _________________ person, attaining to the measure of Christ's full stature. So we are no longer to be _________________, tossed back and forth by waves and carried about by every wind of teaching by the trickery of people who craftily carry out their deceitful schemes. But _________________ the truth in love, we will in all things grow up into Christ, who is the head."

Peace for the Journey

Father, thank you for loving me enough to equip me for the plans you have for my life. Teach me to walk in your purpose and according to your will as you have prepared me. In the name of Jesus Christ, I pray. Amen.

THE GIFT OF PEACE
THAT BINDS US

Reading the Word

> I, therefore, the prisoner for the Lord, urge you to live worthily of the calling with which you have been called, with all humility and gentleness, with patience, putting up with one another in love, making every effort to keep the unity of the Spirit in the bond of peace. There is one body and one Spirit, just as you too were called to the one hope of your calling, one Lord, one faith, one baptism, one God and Father of all, who is over all and through all and in all. (Ephesians 4:1–6 NET)

Living Word by Word

One of my favorite old hymns is "Blest Be the Ties That Bind" by John Fawcett, DD (1739–1817). The hymn describes the relationship of spiritual unity within the body of Christ. The verses proclaim our fellowship of oneness of heart and mind, the focus of our prayers, our love for one another, how we are called to bear one another's burdens, and our great hope for our eternal future with our Lord Jesus Christ.

The apostle Paul wrote about this spiritual unity in Ephesians 4:1–6. Paul writes about the fellowship believers are to have with one another—living a worthy life together with humility, gentleness, patience, and forbearance toward one another. Paul urges the church to keep the unity of the Spirit. The Spirit named here is the Holy Spirit. Our Savior sent the Holy Spirit to abide with those who believe in him—to be our teacher, counselor, and guide.

In Ephesians 4, Paul wrote about the character (Christlike) traits that encourages unity: humility, gentleness, and patience. Humility is understanding our place in relationship with God and with others. Gentleness is showing godly restraint and compassion toward others. Patience is long-suffering, enduring trials and life situations with hopeful purpose. The godly humility, gentleness, and patience in each of us as believers in Jesus Christ, demonstrated toward one another, bind our hearts together in unity.

In unity, we worship one God and walk together in one faith and we strive to live in a bond of peace.

1. How does the binding relationship we have in the Holy Spirit change the way you relate to other believers? ____

____

____

____

____

2. What are some areas where you believe you can strengthen your walk of unity with other believers? ____

____

____

____

____

Blest Be the Tie That Binds[5]

Blest be the tie that binds
our hearts in Christian love;
the fellowship of kindred minds
is like to that above.

Before our Father's throne
we pour our ardent prayers;
our fears, our hopes, our aims are one,
our comforts and our cares.

We share our mutual woes,
our mutual burdens bear,
and often for each other flows
the sympathizing tear.

---

[5] John Fawcett, DD (1739–1817), "Blest Be the Tie That Binds."

When we are called to part,
it gives us inward pain;
but we shall still be joined in heart,
and hope to meet again.

This glorious hope revives
our courage by the way;
while each in expectation lives
and waits to see the day.

From sorrow, toil, and pain,
and sin, we shall be free;
and perfect love and friendship reign
through all eternity.

Peace for the Journey

Father, thank you for the gift of peace we received when we walk in unity with you and with one another. In the name of Jesus Christ, our Lord. Amen.

THE GIFT OF PEACE THAT ENCOURAGES FORGIVENESS

Reading the Word

> Bearing with one another, and forgiving one another, if anyone has a complaint against another; even as Christ forgave you, so you also *must do.* But above all these things put on love, which is the bond of perfection. And let the peace of God rule in your hearts, to which also you were called in one body; and be thankful. (Colossians 3:13–15 NKJV)

Living Word by Word

In this Colossians 3:13 passage, Paul shared three important principles for peaceful living. The first principle is to bear with one another. In the previous verses, Paul was reminding believers about the true holiness we received that is characteristic of having been raised up in Jesus Christ (Colossians 3:1–11). This newness of life leads to a transformation of our focus, our thoughts, and our conduct. An important component of this transformation is the newness of character that will impact how we relate to and respond to others. Paul pointed out that the new life requires believers to cast off worldly attitudes and ungodly conduct (Colossians 3:8–9) and be clothed in the attitudes and conduct that would mark us as having been redeemed in Jesus Christ (Colossians 3:12).

It is only when we take on the new attitudes and conduct we learn in this passage that we can bear with (show tolerance for) the spiritual immaturity of one another. The biblical principle of showing spiritual tolerance must be filtered through the command to love one another. Worldly tolerance simply appeases the sinful behavior. It accepts the behavior, ignoring the spiritual issues that are present in the individual's life and does not encourage change. Loving tolerance seeks to encourage one another to endeavor for the best (Colossians 3:17) and to strive for spiritual growth and maturity (Philippians 1:27).

The second principle that Paul stated in this Colossians passage is that we are not only to bear with one another, but we also are to forgive one another "if anyone has a complaint against another." Sometimes, the hardest thing to do is forgive, especially if the person who caused the injury is someone whom we regarded highly or had great expectations of their spiritual growth. Paul's inference is that everyone will say or do things for which they will need tolerance and sometimes forgiveness.

The third principle that Paul taught in this passage is that when we forgive one another, the bond of unity is strengthened between us. When we walk in unity as the body of Christ, the peace of God will rule (be the umpire over our thoughts and actions).

Is there someone from whom you need to seek forgiveness or you need to offer forgiveness?

1. Write the name of that person in the space here: _______________________________

2. Ask the Lord to lead to you seek peace with that person. What specific issue do you need to deal with in your own life before seeking peace with this person? Write it here: ____

    ____

    ____

    ____

    ____

3. How will you approach this person? Your plan should be SMART. (Read the scriptures listed below, and complete the verses.)
    *   *Selfless.* "See that no one renders ______________ for ______________ to anyone, but always ______________ what is good both for yourselves and for ______________" (1 Thessalonians 5:15).
    *   *Meaningful.* "So, whether you ______________ or ______________, or whatever you do, do all to the ______________ of ______________" (1 Corinthians 10:31).
    *   *Actionable.* "So whoever knows the ______________ thing to do and ______________ to do it, for him it is ______________" (James 4:17).
    *   *Relevant.* "For though I am ______________ from all men, I have made myself a ______________ to all, that I might win the more" (1 Corinthians 9:19).
    *   *Timely.* "Let us not lose heart in doing ______________, for in due __ we will reap if we do not grow ______________" (Galatians 6:9).

4. Write your plan for seeking/offering forgiveness here: _______________________

____

____

____

Peace for the Journey

Father, thank you for the redemption I have in Jesus Christ. Help me to live by the principles of spiritual tolerance and forgiveness so that I can walk in the bond of unity and peace with my brothers and sisters in the body of Christ. In the name of Jesus Christ, I pray. Amen.

THE GIFT OF PEACE THAT OVERCOMES THE WORLD

Reading the Word

> I have told you these things, so that in me you may have peace. In this world you will have trouble. But take heart! I have overcome the world. (John 16:33 NIV)

Living Word by Word

World peace. For centuries, men have sought a means to bring about world peace. After World War II, the United Nations was founded with this purpose, among other goals, as its charter commitment.[6] In the pursuit of peace, men have actually supported wars in order to set rules that allowed them to impose their own will on the lives of others, in the name of peace.

Yet all the ways that men can devise to achieve world peace do not come close to the peace that our Savior Jesus Christ has already provided for us. In John 16, our Lord was concluding his time of teaching in the upper room after the Passover meal. Jesus knew that he was on his way to the cross, and he wanted to make sure the disciples understood how much they were loved and what a gift he was leaving for them in the Holy Spirit. In the Holy Spirit, we have received a comforter, an encourager, a counselor, and a teacher. It is in the presence of the Holy Spirit that we find peace. But his peace is not like the peace we find in the world.

In the world, people look for peace in circumstances of their own making. We replace one thing for another until we find the something that brings us temporary peace, and then we look for the next thing. Worldly peace is about substitutions. But the peace that Jesus Christ gives begins in our hearts and leads to a transformation of our lives. Whatever circumstance we find ourselves dealing with, the peace of Jesus Christ covers us and reminds

---

[6] https://www.un.org/un70/en/content/history/index.html.

us that all sufficiency is found in him. We don't have to find anything to substitute for his peace.

Read the scriptures below, and write what you learn about the peace of God as you seek to stand for him in the world.

1. 1 Thessalonians 5:23 ____

____

2. Galatians 6:16 ____

____

3. 1 Peter 1:2 ____

____

4. Hebrews 13:20 ____

____

5. James 4:8 ____

____

Peace for the Journey

Father, thank you for the peace that you have given us through your Son Jesus Christ. The peace that abides with us forever in the presence of the Holy Spirit. The unchanging peace that sustains us in every situation of life. In the name of Jesus Christ, I pray. Amen.

THE GIFT OF PEACE—
WHEN THINGS DON'T
GO AS EXPECTED

Reading the Word

> I sought the LORD, and he answered me and rescued me from all my fears. Those who look to him are radiant with joy; their faces will never be ashamed. This poor man cried, and the LORD heard him and saved him from all his troubles. The angel of the LORD encamps around those who fear him and rescues them. (Psalm 34:4–7 CSB)

Living Word by Word

David, the king of Israel is credited as the author of Psalm 34 as a commemoration of how the Lord kept him when he was running from Saul and had sought refuge in Gath. He was hoping for a place where he could find rest, but instead, the Philistine ruler, King Achish, recognized David. In desperate need of a place of solace, David changed his behavior (v. 13) in hopes of being allowed to stay in the city for a while. But the king rejected him, and David left the city.

David's plan did not go the way he expected, and he found himself once again looking for a place of safety for himself and his family. Can you imagine the feeling of disappointment and uncertainty he must have felt? As the leader of his family, he was trying to make decisions to keep them safe and provide for their basic needs of food, clothing, and shelter. But in the implementation of his plans, he encountered a major roadblock—things did not go as expected.

We can relate to David's plight in our own lives. When we are making plans for our education, marriage, starting and growing a family, purchasing a home, building our financial portfolio, or trying to ensure a healthy, stable environment for our loved ones, things sometimes do not go as we expected. We encounter loss—the loss of opportunity to continue our educational path, the loss of a job, loss of financial resources, the loss of a baby before it is born, the death of a loved one, shattered relationships, and even the loss of a marriage.

But just as God has a plan for David to restore him to the throne of Israel, he also has a plan for each of us to be restored to the path he has designed for us (Jeremiah 29:11). Our role is to seek the Lord in the time of challenge, and he will respond to our need with his goodness.

David understood this role. He gave testimony to the goodness of God in Psalm 34:4–7. David wrote the story to remind us that:

- Our God can deliver us from the fear we feel in the time of trouble (v. 4).
- When we seek God in prayer, he will transform our thinking and our attitude, even while we are in the midst of the challenging situation (v. 5).
- When we humbly cry out to him, he will save us out of our troubles (v. 6).
- The Lord will place his protection around us to give us peace in our circumstances and confidence that he is able to deliver us (v. 7).

When we seek the Lord and witness his deliverance in our own circumstances, we can give praise to God as David did in Psalm 34:8: "Oh, taste and see that the LORD is good; Blessed is the man who trusts in Him!"

Read the scriptures below, and fill in the promises of God to protect and deliver you. All verses are from the New Living Translation of the Bible.

1. Isaiah 41:10: "Don't be ___________, for I am with you. Don't be ___________, for I am your God. I will ___________ you and help you. I will ___________ you up with my victorious right hand."
2. 1 Peter 5:7: "Give all your worries and cares to God, for he ___________ about you."
3. Psalm 118:6–9: "The LORD is ___________ me, so I will have no fear. What can mere people do to me? Yes, the LORD is ___________ me; he will help me. I will look in triumph at those who hate me. It is better to take refuge in the LORD than to trust in people. It is better to take refuge in the LORD than to trust in princes."
4. Isaiah 40:31: "But those who trust in the LORD will find new ___________. They will ___________ high on wings like eagles. They will ___________ and not grow weary. They will ___________ and not faint."
5. Romans 8:18: "Yet what we suffer now is nothing compared to the ___________ he will reveal to us later."

Father, thank you for your unfailing promises to provide for us, to protect us, and to deliver us through every situation according to your will, plan, and purpose for our lives. In the name of Jesus Christ, I pray. Amen

THE GIFT OF PEACE IN FAITHFUL LIVING

Reading the Word

> Therefore, strengthen your feeble arms and weak knees. "Make level paths for your feet," so that the lame may not be disabled, but rather healed.
>
> Make every effort to live in peace with everyone and to be holy; without holiness no one will see the Lord. See to it that no one falls short of the grace of God and that no bitter root grows up to cause trouble and defile many. See that no one is sexually immoral, or is godless like Esau, who for a single meal sold his inheritance rights as the oldest son. (Hebrews 12:12–16 NIV)

Living Word by Word

The writer of Hebrews begins Chapter 12 by encouraging the church to continue in the race of faith. He urges believers to keep moving forward in their faith by changing how we run the race. In Hebrews 12:1, we are prompted to remember those who ran the race before us and to take note of their testimony of faith.

This verse highlights two things that we must be aware of and remove as obstacles to our race of faith. First, the weights or those things that hinder your progress. This refers to anything that can cause you to lose focus on the kingdom of God. This includes things like (a) attempting to run the race in your own strength; (b) neglecting to seek God's guidance and direction; (c) giving more time than you should to those who are not interested in the things of God or to those who profess to believe in Jesus Christ but have little interest in spiritual growth; (d) devoting too much of your time pursuing activities that do not strengthen you spiritually; and (e) not being diligent to guard your heart against the ungodly enticements of the world.

Weights also refer to things that may seem good in your life—education and career accomplishments, family goals, possessions, and even the position you hold in your local church. If the good things cause you to take your eyes off Jesus, you must reevaluate where you have placed your priorities and make changes so that your race is not hindered.

The second thing that the writer highlighted is "sin that so easily ensnares us." Running the race of faith requires that the runner be both focused on the goal and discerning of the environment around him. When you fix your eyes on Jesus, the enemy will begin to place every manner of opportunity before you to divert your attention from the path. The enemy's goal is to slow down your spiritual pace, hinder your spiritual growth, and cause you to become discouraged and to lose confidence in your calling of faith. Unconfessed sin becomes a "weight" in your life. Believers have a clear way to set aside sin. First John 1:9 (NIV) gives this assurance: "If we confess our sins, he is faithful and just and will forgive us our sins and purify us from all unrighteousness."

In Hebrews 12:12–16, the writer provides pointers for believers to take action so that they can run with endurance in this race of faith. These verses identify best practices for living faithfully daily:

1. *Be strengthened in the Lord*—v. 12. This verse is a continuation from Hebrews 5–11, which reminds believers that as children of God and citizens of the kingdom of heaven, we will receive chastisement when we stray from the path of our faithful walk in the Lord. But the Lord treats us as sons and daughters whom he loves, and his chastisement is for our good. So we are not to be discouraged but instead, we are strengthened when we are chastised so that we can endure the race of faith.

2. *Choose your path carefully*—v. 13. This verse makes it clear that we are not to be hesitant or uncommitted but confident and determined in our daily spiritual walk so that those who follow us do not stumble or lose heart as they observe our testimony as a witness to the Lord's faithfulness in our lives.

3. *Pursue peace with everyone*—v. 14. Believers in Jesus Christ are called to be ambassadors of peace. Even when the situation seems too chaotic to find a way of peace, peace is what we are to pursue. Seek the Lord's guidance. He is the master of every storm that arises in our lives.

4. *Be diligent in righteous living*—v. 14. Righteous living requires the grace of God. If we are to pursuit righteousness in our thought life, our attitudes, our heart desires, and in our conduct, we must depend on the grace of God to sustain us in every thought, every choice, and every action.

5. *Guard your heart against bitterness*—v. 15. Bitterness is the negative companion fueled by the perception of having been unfairly treated, hurt, having anger, and

having disappointment, to name a few causes. A bitter heart is easy to hide by wearing a mask of false acceptance. Left unconfronted, bitterness leads to being easily offended, a sarcastic attitude, a judgmental spirit, poor self-esteem, lack of self-confidence, and the inability to develop healthy relationships. The Bible provides a way to overcome the issues that can lead to bitterness in Matthew 5:23–24 and Matthew 18:15. Be forgiving and seek forgiveness so that you are not tempted to make sinful choices regarding your conduct toward another person.

6. *Be careful of what things you choose to hold in high value*—vv. 16–17. It is sometimes said that life is a series of compromises. We trade the good for the better and the better for the best. Some people choose to live in a way that people will see them as a "good" person by the world's standards, but they neglect the commands of God that would help them to grow as a faithful follower of Jesus Christ. Christians are called to be peculiar people (1 Peter 2:9); therefore, being a good person in the world is not enough. We must pursue being a good citizen of the kingdom of heaven (Philippians 3:20). Instead of compromising to meet the arbitrary standards of a fallen world, put your faith in the things of heaven which cannot be shaken and will not fail (Hebrews 12:28–29).

How can we live faithfully as citizen of the kingdom of heaven? Read the following scriptures and add your insights below:

1. Seek the Lord's help and guidance in your prayer life (James 1:5, Matthew 7:7–12, Mark 11:24, Philippians 4:6–7). _______________________________________
____
____
____
____

2. Read the Word of God daily (Psalm 119:105, Romans 15:4, Hebrews 4:12, 2 Timothy 3:16). ____
____
____
____
____

3. Apply the Word of God to your daily living (Ephesians 5:15–21, Ephesians 5:1, 1 John 2:1–2). ____

____

____

____

4. Seek a godly community that can aid your spiritual growth (Hebrews 10:24–25, 2 Thessalonians 3:6, 2 Corinthians 6:14, Matthew 18:20). _______________________

____

____

____

He has told you, O man, what is good, and what the Lord really wants from you:

He wants you to carry out justice, to love faithfulness, and to live obediently before your God. (Micah 6:8 NET)

Peace for the Journey

Father, thank you for your provision of peace in our lives as we walk faithfully in fellowship with you. In the name of Jesus Christ, I pray. Amen.

THE GIFT OF PEACE THAT FLOWS IN ABUNDANCE

Reading the Word

Mercy, peace, and love be yours in abundance. (Jude 1:2 NIV)

Living Word by Word

I love to read the many prayers of blessing that are included in the word of God. Prayers of blessing call on the power, protection, and provision of God in a specific area of need and often for a particular set of circumstances. The prayer may precede a warning of a specific danger or a word of encouragement to the believers as they are living in distressing time.

Jude 1:2 is a prayer of blessing to the church even as he was warning them about false teachers who had infiltrated the church. Jude's letter is a call to the believers to rise up and be on alert and discerning of those who were teaching a false gospel. Jude urged the believers to recognize the enemy within the camp by their character:

(1) They were deceitful. Jude 4 stated that they "crept in unnoticed." These false teachers managed to blend among the true believers because their message sounded so similar to what the true believers already knew in Jesus Christ.
(2) They were ungodly. Again, in Jude 4, we learn that these false teachers were abusing the grace of God, rejecting the authority of Jesus Christ in their lives, and leading immoral lifestyles. This was a lot for the young church to deal with, and Jude's warning to the church was to keep them from being drawn away from the truth by the glittering worldliness of the false teachers.

In this current age, there are many who have created their own brand of "gospel" that refutes the need for the grace of God, salvation in Jesus Christ, and repentance of sin. They are good at the "razzle-dazzle," and they make millions of dollars in marketing and selling their false teaching. Remember that Jude's warning in just a single chapter to be alert and discerning (1 Peter 5:8–9). Jude encourages us in verse 2 to embrace the mercy, peace, and love of God that is ours in abundance as we walk faithfully with the Lord in the truth of his word.

The writer Jude opened this one-chapter book in our Bible with a prayer of blessing, and he closed with another prayer of blessing that can lift our hearts with a promise of a glorious future in fellowship with the coming king, our Savior.

> Now to the one who is able to keep you from falling, and to cause you to stand, rejoicing, without blemish before his glorious presence, to the only God our Savior through Jesus Christ our Lord, be glory, majesty, power, and authority, before all time, and now, and for all eternity. Amen. (Jude 24–25 NET)

Nine ways the Lord keeps us from stumbling so he can present us as faultless in the day of his coming:

1. Psalm 55:22 ESV: He takes on our burdens—"Cast your burden on the Lord, and he will ___________ you; he will never permit the righteous to be ___________."
2. Psalm 73:26 ESV: He gives more strength—"My flesh and my heart may fail, but God is the ___________ of my heart and my portion forever."
3. Philippians 4:19 ESV: He is our provider—"And my God will ___________ every need of yours according to his riches in glory in Christ Jesus."
4. Psalm 84:11 NIV: He is our protector—"For the LORD God is a sun and ___________; the LORD bestows favor and honor; no good thing does he withhold from those whose walk is blameless."
5. John 14:27 NIV: He keeps us from fear—"Peace I leave with you; my peace I give you. I do not give to you as the world gives. Do not let your hearts be ___________ and do not be ___________."
6. 2 Thessalonians 3:3 NKJV: He guards our hearts—"But the Lord is ___________, who will ___________ you from the evil one."
7. James 1:5 NKJV: He gives wisdom—"If any of you lacks wisdom, let him ask of God, who gives to all liberally and without reproach, and it will be given to him."
8. Romans 15:13 ESV: He is our hope—"May the God of hope ___________ you with all joy and peace in believing, so that by the ___________ of the Holy Spirit you may abound in hope."
9. Isaiah 41:13 ESV: He is our help— "For I, the LORD your God, ___________ your right hand; it is I who say to you, 'Fear not, I am the one who ___________ you.'"

Father, thank you for your Holy Spirit living in us to help us discern the truth from the deceit of the enemy within and without. Thank you for the mercy, peace, and love that flows to us in abundance through our Savior and Lord. In the name of Jesus Christ, I pray. Amen.

THE GIFT OF PEACE THAT IS PLANTED IN RIGHTEOUSNESS

James 3:1–10; 17–18

I am sometimes amazed at the power of the tongue! Words spoken in haste and sometimes in jest can cut deeply into the mental and emotional well-being and can cause great harm. Ungoverned words can cause discouragement, disappointment, resentment, loss of trust, and reputational damage, just to name a few consequences. Speaking without a disciplined tongue is like scattering feathers in the wind. It will be difficult to recover every word. Our words ought to be fountains of encouragement, even in difficult conversations.

Reading the Word

Not many of you should become teachers, my brothers, and sisters, because you know that we will be judged more strictly. For we all stumble in many ways. If someone does not stumble in what he says, he is a perfect individual, able to control the entire body as well. And if we put bits into the mouths of horses to get them to obey us, then we guide their entire bodies. Look at ships too: Though they are so large and driven by harsh winds, they are steered by a tiny rudder wherever the pilot's inclination directs. So too the tongue is a small part of the body, yet it has great pretensions. Think how small a flame sets a huge forest ablaze. And the tongue is a fire! The tongue represents the world of wrongdoing among the parts of our bodies. It pollutes the entire body and sets fire to the course of human existence—and is set on fire by hell. For every kind of animal, bird, reptile, and sea creature is subdued and has been subdued by humankind. But no human being can subdue the tongue; it is a restless evil, full of deadly poison. With it we bless the Lord and Father, and with it we curse people made in God's image. From the same mouth come blessing and cursing. These things should not be so, my brothers and sisters.

But the wisdom from above is first pure, then peaceable, gentle, accommodating, full of mercy and good fruit, impartial, and not hypocritical. And the fruit that consists of righteousness is planted in peace among those who make peace. (James 3:1–10; 17–18 NET)

Living Word by Word

The apostle James focused chapter 3 of the book of James on instructing believers on the importance of godly wisdom to govern the tongue. In James 3:1–12, James wrote about the contrast between an unruly tongue and a governed tongue. James taught about the characteristics of the tongue:

- The tongue can speak words that encourage others or discourage others (vv. 1–4).
- The tongue can speak works that affect the lives of others, either by building them up or by tearing down their reputation (vv. 5–8).
- The tongue can speak words that give harmony or words that lead to chaos (vv. 9–12).

James further stated in verse 13 that the person who is wise will demonstrate wisdom in his or her behavior toward others, and their wisdom will be evident in conversations and the way they govern their tongue. The key to governing the tongue is a heart that seeks the wisdom from God (v. 17). James tells us that this wisdom has distinct traits of godliness.

- First of all, it is pure. There are no hidden motives behind the words spoken in godly wisdom. There is no attempt to manipulate the other person with our words. The speaker is clear and direct, not attempting to cause confusion.
- Secondly, godly wisdom is peaceable. The words spoken in peace can instill confidence, and the speaker has the right motives. These words can give assurance that the speaker does not have a desire to cause a disagreement, division, or disruption.
- Third, godly wisdom leads to humility, kindness, right conduct, and peace. Words spoken in godly wisdom should bring about understanding and reconciliation.

In James 3:18, the word *sown* reminds us of seeds that are scattered in a field. The seeds are true to their origin. The type of seed planted is an indicator of the type of produce that will grow. There is no surprise when the plant grows as to what type of fruit it will bear.

The same is true with the "seeds" of our tongues. If words are spoken in anger or to cause disagreement, we should not be surprised when the hearer responds in anger or becomes disagreeable. But when words are spoken in the pursuit of peace, we can reasonably expect those words to lead to peace.

The apostle's teaching in James chapter 3 echoed other writers in the Bible, who also spoke about the power of the tongue. Read the following verses, and add your insights about these verses in the space provided below:

1. Psalm 141:3 ____
   ____

2. Proverb 15:1____
   ____

3. Proverbs 18:21 ____
   ____

4. Proverbs 25:15 ____
   ____

5. Matthew 12:36–37 ____
   ____

6. Matthew 15:11 ____
   ____

7. 1 Peter 3:10 ____
   ____

8. Colossians 4:6 ____
   ____

Peace for the Journey

Father, thank you for the wisdom of heaven that you give to us so that we know how to govern our hearts and control our tongues. Help us to walk in your godly wisdom in every daily interaction with others so that our words will seed of peace. In the name of Jesus Christ, I pray. Amen.

THE GIFT OF PEACE IN THE LORD'S SAFETY

Reading the Word

> In peace I will lie down and sleep, for you alone, Lord, make me dwell in safety. (Psalm 4:8 NIV)

Living Word by Word

King David, the writer of Psalm chapter 4 was anxious about his well-being and that of the people who were with him. David was threatened by his son Absalom, who attempted to overthrow his father's rulership and replace him as king of Israel. David fled the capital, along with members of his family and some friends. In the midst of this stress and anxiety-filled crisis, it is amazing that David could sleep, but we read in Psalm 3:5–6 that he did sleep because he depended on God as his protector and sustainer. David was able to sleep in peace although others were plotting against him. In Psalm 4:8, we read that David could sleep in peace because he trusted the Lord with his safety.

How awesome is a peaceful night's sleep when you can wake up the next morning refreshed, full of energy, and ready to face a new day! Peaceful rest at night yields many benefits for daily living and well-being. Health professionals say that healthy, restful sleep helps the body to heal from illness or injury. Sleep helps to maintain a strong heart and sustain a healthy blood pressure level. Establishing a consistent, healthy sleeping routine promotes good memory and cognitive thinking ability, helps to decrease stress, and increases metabolism, which helps with weight management. And those are just a few of the physical benefits!

The techniques we use to try to achieve restful sleep are often ineffective because of the underlying issues of stress or anxiety or overactive brain activity or even fear for the future. But in the middle of our life crisis, we can lay down in peace and rest in safety because of our relationship with the Lord. We can depend on our Lord to provide comfort in the time of crisis so we can find rest and refreshment in sleep. Our Lord is committed to our safety and well-being.

Read the following verses, and complete the statements about the peace and safety we have in Jesus Christ. All verses are New King James Version.

1. Psalm 91:1–2: "He who dwells in the ______________ of the Most High will abide in the ____________ of the Almighty. I will say to the LORD, "My ____________ and my ___________, my God, in whom I trust."

2. Proverbs 11:14: "Where there is no guidance, a people falls, but in an ____________ of ____________ there is safety."

3. Psalm 4:8: "In ____________ I will both lie down and sleep; for you alone, O Lord, make me dwell in ____________."

4. 1 John 5:18: "We know that everyone who has been born of God does not keep on sinning, but he who was born of God ____________ him, and the evil one does not ____________ him."

5. Psalm 55:18: "He redeems my soul in ___________ from the battle that I wage, for many are arrayed against me."

6. Job 5:11–12: "He sets on high those who are ___________, and those who ___________ are lifted to ____________. He frustrates the devices of the crafty, so that their hands achieve no success."

7. Psalm 78:53: "He led them in ____________, so that they were not afraid, but the sea overwhelmed their enemies."

Peace for the Journey

Father, thank you for the safety we have in you through Jesus Christ our Savior. Teach us to walk in faith as we trust you to lead us in safety and peace. In the name of Jesus Christ, I pray. Amen.

THE GIFT OF PEACE
IN DAILY CONDUCT

Reading the Word

> Whatever you have learned or received or heard from me or seen in me—put it into practice. And the God of peace will be with you. (Philippians 4:9 NIV)

Living Word by Word

The apostle Paul, in several passages of his writing (Philippians 3:17; 1 Corinthians 11:1, 1 Corinthians 4:16, and Philippians 4:9), encourages believers in Jesus Christ to look to him as an earthly role model of how to follow Jesus Christ in our daily conduct. Paul is not suggesting that we focus on his spiritual walk instead of the Jesus Christ. He is encouraging us to seek out someone who is striving to walk in a way that honors God so that their spiritual talk is modeled in their spiritual walk. Such a person can become role model for those who are also determined to be successful in their walk with Jesus Christ.

What should you look for in a spiritual role model? The Bible provides the guidance for spiritual role models. Spiritual role models are simply believers who demonstrate the godly characteristics we want in our own lives. Read the verses below to learn more about the traits you want to identify in a spiritual role model.

1. One who demonstrates the fruit of the spirit in their conduct—Galatians 5:22–23.
2. One who sets an example of doing good—Titus 2:7.
3. One who offers godly instruction—Proverbs 1:8 and Proverbs 8:33.
4. One who strives to live in harmony with others—Romans 12:16 and Hebrews 12:14–16.
5. One who strives to live in holiness—1 Peter 1:15–16.

6. One who strives to walk by faith—Philippians 4:8; Proverbs 4:23, Isaiah 26:3, and Matthew 12:37.

Peace for the Journey

Father, thank you for the guidance of your Word for our daily conduct. Help us to be discerning in seeking role models who can walk with us to help us walk in godliness in our daily lives. In the name of Jesus Christ, we pray. Amen.

THE GIFT OF PEACE
IN THE FACE OF A
FRIEND'S BETRAYAL

He has redeemed my soul in peace from the battle that was against me, for there were many against me. (Psalm 55:18)

Reading the Word

Indeed, it is not an enemy who insults me, or else I could bear it; it is not one who hates me who arrogantly taunts me, or else I could hide from him. But it is you, a man like me, my close friend in whom I confided. We would share personal thoughts with each other; in God's temple we would walk together among the crowd. (Psalm 55:12–14 NET)

Living Word by Word

Have you ever been betrayed by a friend—someone you trusted and with whom you shared personal hopes and dreams, life challenges, and successes? The person you counted on to have your back, who would go the extra mile for you and you for them. Your ride or die partner until you find out that they didn't really have your best interest at heart.

The betrayal of a friend is one of the most hurtful experiences we face in life. The shock of such betrayal is almost too much to believe. The experience disrupts our emotional well-being and our spiritual peace. In Psalm 55:12–14, David was writing about a friend he had worshipped alongside in the temple, who was his trusted advisor, and whom he had previously trusted with his life, but who he discovered was conspiring to take his life (2 Samuel 15:12).

How can we honor God in our response to a friend's betrayal? Forgiveness is not easy, but it is possible. The Bible offers a relationship map for our guidance.

1. *Seek the peace of God*: Isaiah 26:3—"You will keep him in perfect peace, whose mind is stayed on you, because he trusts in you."
2. *Pray*: James 5:16—"So confess your sins to one another and pray for one another so that you may be healed. The prayer of a righteous person has great effectiveness."
   - Pray it through with God concerning your own heart condition.
   - Pray it through with God concerning your friend's behavior.
3. *Do not be lured into the enemy's (Satan) trap of revenge*: 1 Peter 5:8—"Be alert and of sober mind. Your enemy the devil prowls around like a roaring lion looking for someone to devour." The enemy of your soul will tell you that you deserve to be avenged for the wrong done to you. But remember, God is the judge and the one who delivers justice (Psalm 55:16–18).
4. *Forgive*: Colossians 3:13—"Bear with each other and forgive one another if any of you has a grievance against someone. Forgive as the Lord forgave you."
5. *Be reconciled*: Ephesians 4:31—"Get rid of all bitterness, rage and anger, brawling and slander, along with every form of malice." The relationship may never be the same, but it does not have to be antagonistic either. As followers of Jesus Christ, we are called to reconciliation so that we can share the good news of the kingdom of God. We cannot be a beacon of light, pointing the way toward the Lord while we are also holding a dagger of resentment.
   - Is there someone in your life who has betrayed your friendship? ____________
   ____
   ____

   - What are some needs that you know that person has in their life that you can pray about right now for God's will to intervene on their behalf? ____________
   ____
   ____

Peace for the Journey

Father, teach me to walk in an attitude of forgiveness for those who I hold dear and who have betrayed me. Teach me how to pray for them and to forgive them by the same measure that you have forgiven me. In the name of Jesus Christ, I pray. Amen.

THE GIFT OF PEACE THAT CAN MAKE YOUR SPIRIT WHOLE

Reading the Word

> Now may the God of peace Himself sanctify you completely; and may your whole spirit, soul, and body be preserved blameless at the coming of our Lord Jesus Christ. (1 Thessalonians 5:23 NKJV)

Living Word by Word

One of my favorite old African American spirituals is the hymn "There Is a Balm in Gilead."[7]

Chorus:
There is a balm in Gilead
To make the wounded whole
There is a balm in Gilead
To heal the sin-sick soul.

Verse 1:
Sometimes I feel discouraged
And think my work's in vain,
But then the Holy Spirit
Revives my soul again.

---

[7] "A Balm in Gilead," Psalter Hymnal (Gray) (1987).

Verse 2:
If you cannot preach like Peter,
If you cannot pray like Paul,
You can tell the love of Jesus
And say, "He died for all."

The verses of this song remind me that no matter how difficult the situation and how overwhelmed I may feel, the Holy Spirit is able to revive my spirit and restore me to wholeness in mind, body, soul, and spirit. The song is an encourager for the one who faces opposition while trying to live a life pleasing to God and is still holding on to hope and peace in Jesus Christ.

The apostle Paul offered a similar encouraging prayer for the church at Thessalonica as he wrote to encourage the members of this Gentile church in their faith walk while they faced opposition from the Jews and others who were opposed to the preaching of the gospel in that city. But the believers clung to Jesus, and the city became a hub for the evangelistic effort in that region (1 Thessalonians 1:6–8).

Paul offered some godly advice to the Thessalonians for how to live in "wholeness." Complete the statements below with his advice. All verses are from the New King James Version of the Bible.

1. 1 Thessalonians 4:1—"Finally then, brethren, we urge and exhort in the Lord Jesus that you should ____________ more and more, just as you received from us how you ought to ____________ and to please God."
2. 1 Thessalonians 5:18—"In everything give thanks; for this is the ____________ of God in Christ Jesus for you."
3. 1 Thessalonians 5:15—"See that no one renders evil for evil to anyone, but always __________ what is good both for yourselves and for all."
4. 1 Thessalonians 5:16—"____________________ always."
5. 1 Thessalonians 5:17—"____________________ without ceasing."
6. 1 Thessalonians 4:16—"For the Lord Himself will ____________ from heaven with a shout, with the voice of an archangel, and with the trumpet of God. And the ______________ in Christ will rise first."
7. 1 Thessalonians 5:11—"Therefore comfort each other and edify one another, just as you also are doing."

Father, thank you for your Holy Spirit, who is the comforter of my soul. I pray that as I walk in the Spirit, I will grow in wholeness. In the name of Jesus Christ, I pray. Amen

THE PEACE OF GOD THAT JOINS US TOGETHER

For He Himself is our peace, who has made both one, and has broken down the middle wall of separation. (Ephesians 2:14 NKJV)

Reading the Word

Therefore remember that formerly you, the Gentiles in the flesh—who are called "uncircumcision" by the so-called "circumcision" that is performed on the body by human hands—that you were at that time without the Messiah, alienated from the citizenship of Israel and strangers to the covenants of promise, having no hope and without God in the world. But now in Christ Jesus you who used to be far away have been brought near by the blood of Christ. *For he is our peace, the one who made both groups into one and who destroyed the middle wall of partition, the hostility,* when he nullified in his flesh the law of commandments in decrees. He did this to create in himself one new man out of two, thus making peace, and to reconcile them both in one body to God through the cross, by which the hostility has been killed. And he came and preached peace to you who were far off and peace to those who were near, so that through him we both have access in one Spirit to the Father. So then you are no longer foreigners and noncitizens, but you are fellow citizens with the saints and members of God's household, because you have been built on the foundation of the apostles and prophets, with Christ Jesus himself as the cornerstone. In him the whole building, being joined together, grows into a holy temple in the Lord, in whom you also are being built together into a dwelling place of God in the Spirit. (Ephesians 2:11–22 NET)

In current times and culture, we are overwhelmed by the many factions that seem to endlessly struggle for political power, control, and attention because of their self-proclaimed "rights." The struggle spills over from the world and into the *church*—the body of Christ, where politics has gained a foothold in a place and among people where only the Word of God must rule. The result is that walls of separation—based on traditional, personal, and cultural preferences—are sometimes built up in local communities and in what ought to be God-fearing congregations and among people groups and in families. The walls keep Christians from loving God, loving people, and serving people as one body in Jesus Christ. This wall was torn down and destroyed by our Savior through his great sacrifice on the cross. Ephesians 2 tells us that he destroyed the wall and he came and preached peace that unites us in one body, with access in one Spirit to the Father. But self-pride and selfish ambition had led many believers to return to rebuild the wall of separation by replacing the truth of the Bible with the "truths" of our preferences.

Our Lord still calls us to return to him and keep our eyes on him so that we do not miss where he is working. Read the verses below to recall how he is working as he prepares us for his coming.

1. Philippians 2:13—He is working in us.
2. Ephesians 2:10—He is working through us.
3. 1 Corinthians 3:9—He is working with us.

Peace for the Journey

Father, thank you for tearing down the wall of separation that kept believers from loving and serving together. We pray for the guidance of the Holy Spirit so that we do not attempt to sift the truth of the Word through the filters of the world. Help us to keep our focus on you so that we are not putting up new walls based on our own flawed understanding.

THE GIFT OF PEACE
THAT BLESSES

Reading the Word

> And the LORD spoke to Moses, saying: "Speak to Aaron and his sons, saying, 'This is the way you shall bless the children of Israel. Say to them: The LORD bless you and keep you; The LORD make His face shine upon you And be gracious to you; The LORD lift up His countenance upon you And give you peace.'
>
> So they shall put my name on the children of Israel, and I will bless them." (Numbers 6:22–27 NKJV)

Living Word by Word

What a blessing it is to speak words of blessing over others!

After the Israelites had come through their journey to their promised home, the Lord gave Moses the laws that would govern how the people would honor God and how they would live together as the people of God. He established government (Romans 13:1–2) and community (Numbers 2). He appointed priests to lead the people in worship and honoring God, and he appointed those who were to be workers in the tabernacle to maintain and safeguard the place of his dwelling (Numbers 3–5). And in Numbers 6:22–26, he poured out his loving kindness in a blessing over the people. This blessing is not just a general "God bless you."

The Hebrew word *bârakh* is translated in English "to bless." The meaning of this word refers to God's faithful provision for his children. He is detailed in his blessings toward us, providing for all our needs. The blessings of the Lord do not fall short but meet every need we have.

This blessing is also for the protection of the Lord. The Hebrew word *shamar*, which means to guard and protect, is translated in English to the word *keep*. The blessing of Aaron over the people offers God's provision and protection for God's people. In Numbers 6:26, the blessing asks that God will show his continuing favor toward the children by covering their lives with his grace and peace.

In Deuteronomy 28:1–14, the Lord describes the blessings that he will pour out on Israel if they diligently obey his commands. Read this passage (taken from the New Living Translation of the Bible), and complete the statements below:

1. Verse 3: "Your _____________ and your _____________ will be blessed."
2. Verse 4: "Your _____________ and your _____________ you will be blessed." The _____________ of your herds and flocks will be blessed."
3. Verse 5: "Your _____________ baskets and _____________ will be blessed."
4. Verse 6: "Wherever you _____________ and whatever you _____________, you will be blessed.
5. Verse 7: "The LORD will _____________ your enemies when they attack you."
6. Verse 8: "The LORD will _____________ a blessing on everything you do and will fill your storehouses with grain. The LORD your God will bless you in the _____________ he is giving you."
7. Verse 9: "If you obey the commands of the LORD your God and walk in his ways, the LORD will _____________ you as his holy people as he swore he would do."
8. Verse 10: "Then all the nations of the world will see that you are a people _____________ by the LORD, and they will stand in awe of you."
9. Verse 11: "The LORD will give you _____________ in the land he swore to your ancestors to give you."
10. Verse 12: "The LORD will send rain at the _____________ time from his rich _____________ in the heavens and will bless all the work you do. You will _____________ to many nations, but you will never need to _____________ from them."
11. Verse 13: "If you listen to these commands of the LORD your God that I am giving you today, and if you carefully obey them, the LORD will make you the _____________ and not the _____________, and you will always be on _____________ and never at the _____________."

When we pronounce blessings over others, we are speaking the power of the Holy Spirit to do great work in their lives based on the Word of God (Philippians 4:19). We are seeking God's provision for their needs, protection as they face a challenge, or the peace of God so that they will have faith and confidence to endure. We speak blessings to encourage others, but we also are blessed by our strengthened faith that our Lord will act on their behalf.

Father, thank you for the blessings that you have poured out on all who believe in you. Help us to demonstrate your love by speaking blessings according to your Word over the lives of others to impact encouragement, assurance, and peace. In the name of Jesus Christ, I pray. Amen.

ABOUT THE AUTHOR

Doris Willis has served as a Christian teacher, ministry leader, workshop leader, and conference speaker. She currently serves as the women's ministry director and as a Bible teacher. One of her greatest joys is seeing others grow deeper in fellowship with the Lord through ministering, mentoring, teaching, and developing others using the message of the Gospel, as well as guiding others to discover their spiritual gifts and engage in ministry. Doris is a native Texan and enjoys gardening, cooking, and spending time with her husband of thirty-seven years and their two adult sons and their families, and being "GranGran" to her grandchildren.